S0-BSR-184

THE WORLD BEYOND EARTH
UNMANNED EXPLORERS AND ORBITERS

CONTENTS

WHAT TO DO

YOU MIGHT NEED:

- a dictionary
- a thesaurus
- an atlas

NOW:

- choose a face
- when you see your face, you are the leader
- when you are the leader, follow these steps:

1. Predict

Say to your group:
"I think this page is going to be about..."

You can use these things to help you predict:

- photographs
- captions
- headings
- what you already know

Tell your group to read the page silently.

2. Clarify

When your group has finished reading, ask them if there is anything they don't understand.
Say: *"Is there anything anyone doesn't understand?"*

It could be:
- a word
- something someone has read

3. Ask Questions

Ask your group if anyone would like to ask a question about what they have read.
Say: *"Does anyone have a question they would like to ask?"*

4. Summarize

Now... you can tell your group what the main ideas are on this page.
Say: *"I think this page has been about..."*

UNMANNED EXPLORERS AND ORBITERS

I predict this is going to be about...

People have always wondered about the mysteries of space. What lies beyond Earth – the Moon, the stars, the planets, the unknown – has captured our imaginations for thousands of years.

There were many things that people believed to explain what they saw when they looked in the sky. Some ancient people believed that Earth floated in a glass ball, which was hung from the top of an enormous mountain. They thought that anyone who could climb high enough up one of Earth's mountains would be able to touch the inside of the glass ball.

Today, we know much more about space because humans have traveled there. Yet our understanding comes from more than people spending time in space. Specially designed equipment, and even highly trained animals, are used to explore and investigate the fascinating universe beyond Earth.

Does anyone need to have anything clarified?

An unmanned orbiter – the Hubble Space Telescope

Ancient people believed that the Earth might be inside a glass ball.

Does anyone have a question to ask?

My summary of what we have read is...

ANIMALS IN SPACE

I predict this is going to be about...

In the early days of space travel, scientists knew nothing about how people would survive traveling there. Scientists decided to send animals into space to learn about the conditions humans might face once they left the safety of the Earth.

By studying the animals, the scientists were able to test what it was like to live without Earth's gravity and atmosphere. The animals were used to test equipment that would later be used for human space flight. Animals that survived a space flight provided information about how weightlessness would affect humans, what cabin designs would be safest, and how well a space suit would work.

Dogs were the most common animal sent into space. They were good because their size, breathing patterns, and blood flow are similar to humans.

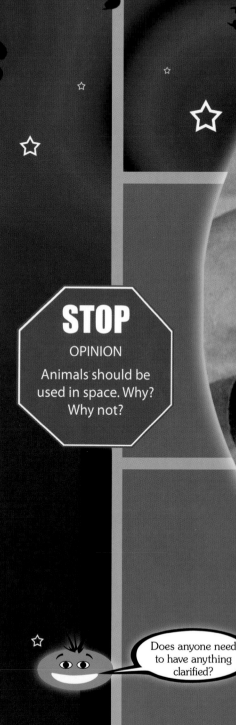

STOP

OPINION

Animals should be used in space. Why? Why not?

Does anyone need to have anything clarified?

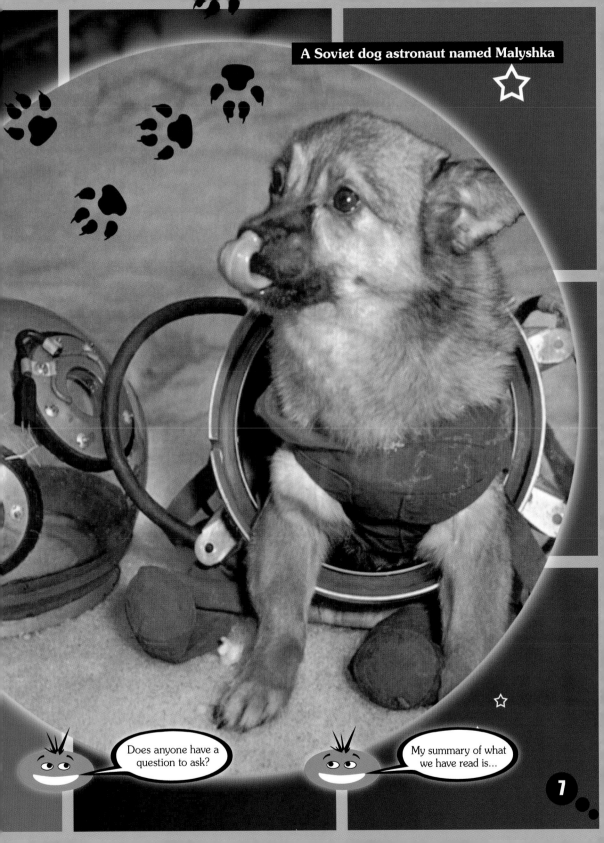

I predict this is going to be about...

Scientists have used other kinds of animals for space-travel experiments. Chimpanzees were sent into space because of their similarities to humans, and because they could be trained to perform tasks. Frogs orbited Earth to provide information for scientists on how the inner ear works. These flights helped scientists understand motion sickness. Monkeys, rats, mice, flies, fish, ants, snails, beetles, sea urchins, and hundreds of jellyfish are all animals that have traveled in space.

Today, an animal is chosen for space travel based on the experiment that needs to be done. There are now very strict rules about taking animals into space. They must be treated with great care, and many people feel that animals should not be used in this way at all.

Preparing a chimpanzee for space travel

Frogs helped scientists understand how the inner ear works.

Does anyone have a question to ask?

My summary of what we have read is...

9

ANIMAL REACTIONS IN SPACE

I predict this is going to be about…

Animals have reacted to space travel in different ways. Scientists found that fish and tadpoles swam in loops rather than in straight lines. It was difficult for some baby mammals to get used to being in space because they drifted apart from each other. On Earth they were used to huddling together for comfort and warmth. A comb of honeybees that were taken into space didn't know what to do at first. However, they did adjust, and they soon built a hive just like they would have on Earth.

Mice adapted very quickly when they traveled on a spacecraft. After just a few minutes, they were floating in space, behaving almost the same as they would on Earth.

Animals gave scientists the information needed to launch human space travel. Sadly, though, many also gave their lives.

STOP

When you read, "fish and tadpoles swam in loops," what picture do you get in your head?

Does anyone need to have anything

Tadpoles

Does anyone have a
question to ask?

My summary of what
we have read is...

SENT FROM EARTH
DEEP SPACE PROBES

I predict this is going to be about...

Deep space probes are spacecraft that have many instruments on board, but no people. They are launched into space just like a rocket is, but they have more power than a rocket. Deep space probes need more power to push past the pull of Earth's gravity and allow them to move great distances to explore other planets in the solar system.

Scientists enter most directions for the probe into its computer before it leaves Earth. Sometimes, though, changes have to be made once the probe is in space. Scientists can send changes to the probe's onboard computer from Earth – even though the probe may be millions of miles away! Space probes are used to send scientists information from space environments that are beyond the reach of human astronauts, or are too dangerous for normal spacecraft.

Does anyone need to have anything clarified?

STOP

OPINION

It is important for us to find out information about our solar system. Why? Why not?

Jupiter and *Galileo*

Boeing *Delta II* launches into space, carrying the *Gravity Probe B*.

Does anyone have a question to ask?

My summary of what we have read is...

WHAT A DEEP SPACE PROBE DOES

I predict this is going to be about...

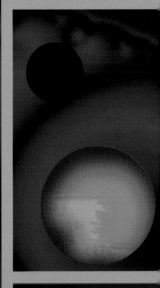

Deep space probes have orbited around nearly every planet in Earth's solar system, visited several asteroids, and flown by comets, collecting samples. The first space probe to escape Earth's gravity was *Luna 1*. *Luna 1* shot past the Moon, and instead ended up orbiting the Sun. However, it did provide valuable information about outer space. It showed that there was no magnetic field around the Earth's Moon, and that there was a solar wind in space.

Some space probes can be directed to actually land on planets and moons. Before astronauts could land on the Moon, space probes were sent to see if it would be possible. One probe had a shovel that dug into the surface of the Moon to see how deep the dust was. If the dust were too deep, then astronauts would not have been able to land there.

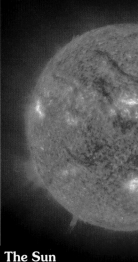

The Sun

Does anyone need to have anything clarified?

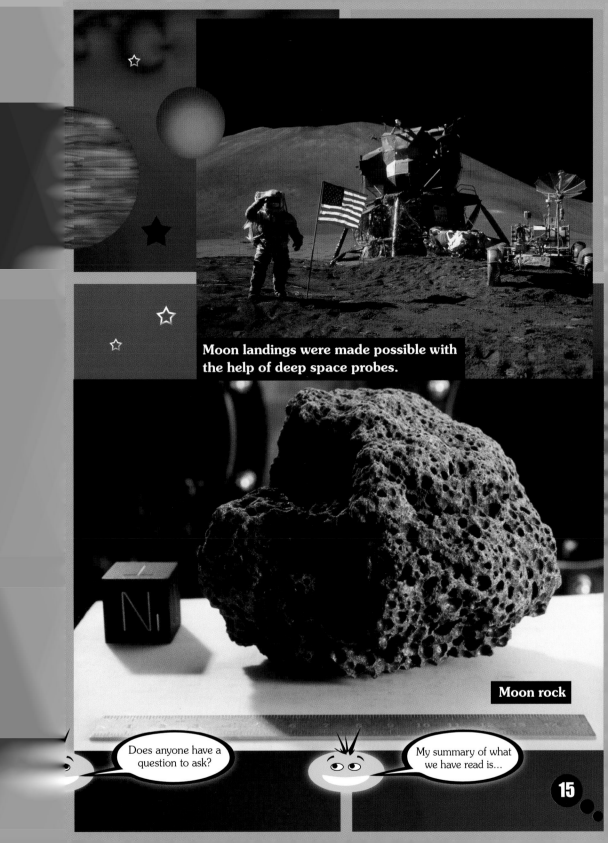

Moon landings were made possible with the help of deep space probes.

Moon rock

Does anyone have a question to ask?

My summary of what we have read is...

SPACE PROBES ON MARS

I predict this is going to be about...

The planet Mars has fascinated people for centuries. One of the main questions about Mars is whether there might be life on its dusty surface. Scientists believe that, next to Earth, Mars is the most likely planet to support life. To explore the mysteries of the "red planet," U.S. scientists sent two space probes to land on Mars and find out whether simple life could exist there. These probes measured gases in the air and chemicals in the soil, but they didn't find any signs of life.

Other space probes that have been sent to Mars have carried robotic rovers. These rovers travel around the surface of Mars, collecting scientific evidence. A camera records what they find and sends the pictures back to scientists on Earth.

Space probes are an ideal way to explore space because they can reach places that humans can't.

STOP
What connections can you make with finding information about something?

Does anyone need to have anything clarified?

16

A robotic rover

Mars lander collecting samples

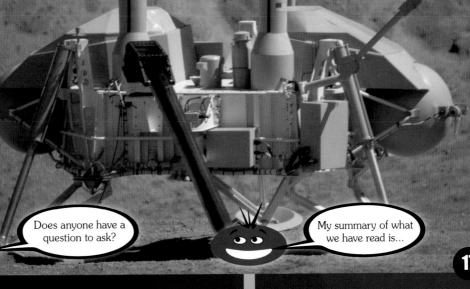

ORBITING SATELLITES

I predict this is going to be about…

Closer to Earth, in the space all around it, there are many objects orbiting the planet. These are called satellites. There are both natural and artificial satellites. The Earth's Moon is a natural satellite. Other planets have satellites too. The planet Saturn has more than thirty satellites, or moons, orbiting it!

Other than orbiting the Earth, artificial satellites don't have much in common with natural ones. They are built by people to do a wide range of jobs. Some help gather and send information. They help people forecast the weather, and they can relay telephone calls all over the world. Signals from satellites even give many people their TV service!

Satellites can be amazingly powerful. Even though a satellite might be hundreds of miles above Earth, it can photograph a bird in a tree, or measure the height of an ocean wave.

Earth's Moon

Does anyone need to have anything

Satellite orbiting the Earth

Photo of a hurricane taken by a weather satellite orbiting Earth

19

SPACE JUNK

I predict this is going to be about...

After a while, all satellites stop working. Some completely burn up in space, but others don't. They become space junk.

Space junk is any human-made garbage that is left out in space. This junk zooms around the planet at speeds of up to 25,000 miles per hour. Although space junk is mostly small, its high speed can make it a threat to spacecraft. Even a tiny piece of paint could cause serious damage if it were to smack into a speeding rocket. Scientists on Earth can track pieces of space junk that are baseball-size or bigger, and space junk falling back into the Earth's atmosphere can light up the sky like a natural meteor.

Some space junk that zooms around:
nuts
bolts
gloves
old satellites
space probes
garbage
remains of rockets

Nuts and bolts zoom at 25,000 mph!

Does anyone need to have anything clarified?

STOP

When you read, "junk zooms around the planet," what picture do you get in your head?

Satellites run the risk of crashing into space junk as they orbit the Earth.

Does anyone have a question to ask?

My summary of what we have read is...

SPACE JUNK ON PLANETS

I predict this is going to be about...

Space junk has even been left on Earth's Moon and on planets. On the Moon, there are thousands of pounds of it. There are old Moon buggies, parts of rockets, and even some golf balls! Some astronauts have left behind things they didn't need because they had to make room in their spacecraft for Moon samples. Astronauts have left things such as flags to let others know that they have been there.

Probes have also left space junk on Mars and Venus.

Space junk that is left on planets could one day become a space museum – or even a treasure.

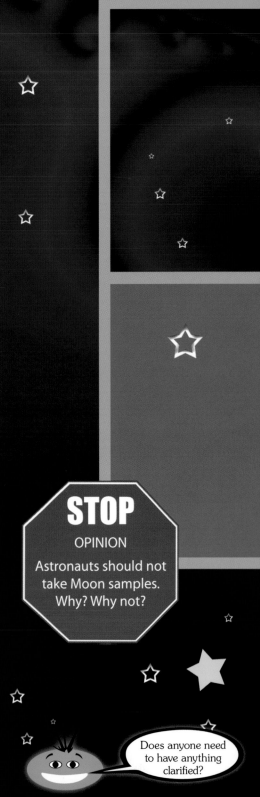

STOP
OPINION
Astronauts should not take Moon samples. Why? Why not?

Does anyone need to have anything clarified?

TELESCOPES –
SPACE EYES

I predict this is going to be about...

Space telescopes are satellites in space that gather information about things, such as distant stars and galaxies, that have never been seen before. Space telescopes can take thousands of pictures a day. The Hubble Telescope, launched in 1990, collects pictures and information and then sends it another 90,000 miles to scientists on Earth.

Space telescopes are the "space eyes" of scientists. They allow scientists to see amazing images of deep space. Through telescopes, scientists have seen galaxies that are billions of light-years away. They have seen new stars forming – and maybe even other, ancient solar systems!

Space telescopes such as the Hubble can allow scientists to gaze back billions of years in time.

STOP

When you read, "gaze back billions of years in time," what picture do you get in your head?

Does anyone need

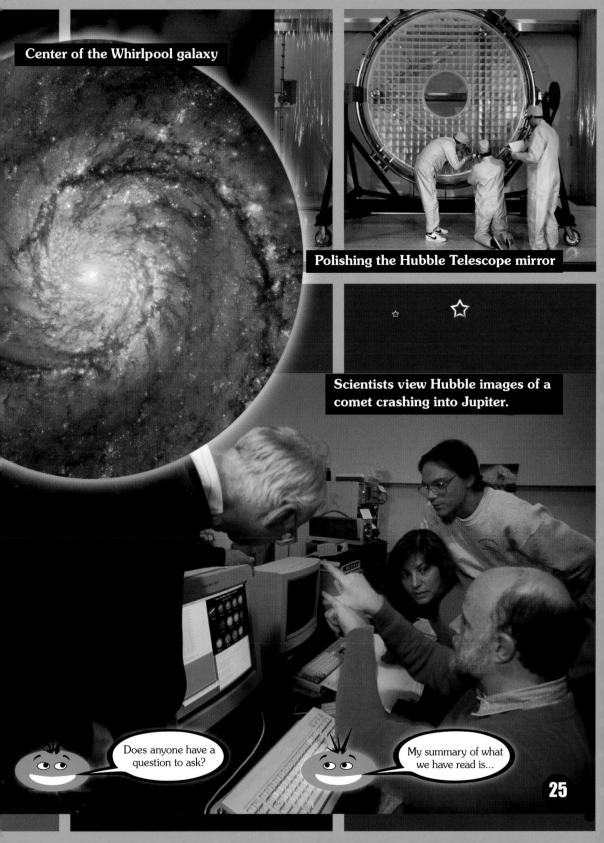

Center of the Whirlpool galaxy

Polishing the Hubble Telescope mirror

Scientists view Hubble images of a comet crashing into Jupiter.

WHAT NEXT?

I predict this is going to be about...

Scientists are always trying to venture to new places, to reach out farther into space. They are trying to invent new ways to explore the world beyond Earth.

Could these dreams become real?

A Space Elevator
An elevator on a cable stretching from Earth to a planet

A Solar Sail
A rocket moving through space with no engine but with huge, wafer-thin sails

What next will be exploring, orbiting, and showing us the world beyond Earth?

A solar sail

Does anyone have a question to ask?

My summary of what we have read is...

SOMETHING TO THINK ABOUT

PMI

PLUS	MINUS	INTERESTING
Animals could test whether a human could survive in space.	The animals may suffer.	Chimpanzees were sent into space because of their similarities to humans.

PMI

PLUS	MINUS	INTERESTING
Space probes can explore places that aren't safe for humans.	They can get lost and become space junk.	Space probes could be used on Earth.

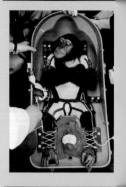

TELESCOPES

ANIMALS
IN SPACE

The World Beyond Earth

SENT FROM EARTH

SPACE
JUNK

Try searching in books and on the Internet
using these key words to help you:

astronauts
galaxies
orbiting objects
planets
satellites
solar sail
space animals
space discovery
space elevator
space inventions
space junk
space telescopes

INDEX